Farms
Around the World

written by Kelly Gaffney

There are farms all around the world.

Most of the food that we eat comes from farms.

Other things that we use every day
can come from farms, too.

Some farms have plants, and other farms have animals.

There are farms in many different places.

Some farms are in beautiful green *fields*.

Others are in places that are hot and dusty.

There are even farms that are in water!

Some farms are very large, while others are very small.

But all farms are really important to us.

Plant Farms

Plants that grow on farms are called *crops*.
Some farmers grow many different crops,
while other farmers grow only one crop.

Crops are often planted in long rows
to let the farmer drive a tractor between them.
This makes it easy to care for the crops
and pick them when they are ready to sell.

Some farmers grow *vegetables* such as peas, corn and potatoes. Other farmers grow *fruit* such as apples, plums and oranges.

Farms can also be used to grow rice.

Rice needs lots of water to grow.

Farmers grow rice in a special pond called a *rice paddy*.

Some rice paddies are made by covering fields with water.

A rice paddy can also be dug into the side of a hill.

Farmers in some parts of the world use *water buffalo* to help them work in their rice paddies.

rice paddy

rice

A farmer with a water buffalo.

Animal Farms

Many farms have animals.

Some farmers keep sheep on their farms.

Sheep are kept so that a farmer can sell their wool.

Wool can be made into lots of things,
such as clothes and blankets.

A farmer looks after the sheep while their wool grows
long and thick.

Then the sheep are rounded up and their wool is cut off.

Cutting off a sheep's wool is called *shearing*.

It doesn't hurt the sheep, and their wool grows back
very quickly.

Did you know?

Sometimes dogs are trained to help round up the sheep.

Farms that have cattle on them
are sometimes called *ranches*.
Ranches need to be large so that there is plenty
of grass for the cattle.
The farmer has to move the cattle from one place
to another so that they always have enough food.

bull

cow

calf

There are also farms that keep cows for their milk.
Cow's milk can be used to make
butter, cream and cheese.
It can be used to make ice cream, too.

Farmers can use their hands to milk a cow,
but most farmers use special *machines*
because it's much quicker.

Did you know?

Farms that have cows
to milk are called
dairy farms.

Did you know?

Getting milk from
a cow is called "milking".

There are many other things that come from farms.
Most of the beautiful flowers sold in shops
grow on farms.
The *cotton* used to make our clothes
comes from farms, too.
And even some of the fish we eat comes from farms.

If you were a farmer, what would you like
to have on your farm?

flowers

cotton

fish farm

15

Picture glossary

cotton

fields

ranches

vegetables

crops

fruit

rice paddy

water buffalo

dairy

machines

shearing

wheat